Contents

Words that appear in **bold** are explained in the glossary.

What Are Rocks?

You may not notice it, but nearly everything you stand on is made of rock! This is because the outer layer of our Earth is made of rock. There is even rock under forests and oceans.

There are many different kinds of rocks. They can be very hard, or powdery, or soft and easy to mold. Rocks can be many different colours, shapes and sizes.

Rocks can form big mountains.

Sand is made up of tiny rocks.

It's a Fact!

Sand is a type of rock. When it is heated, it can be made into glass.

The Twelve Apostles, Victoria, Australia

Rocks shape all the landscapes around us. See how many different kinds of rocks you discover next time you are out in the countryside or by the sea.

We use rocks to make things, too. Roads, buildings and statues are all made of different kinds of rocks. The plates you eat from and the chalks you draw with are made of rock, too!

How Do Rocks Form?

Rocks are forming and changing all the time. This sometimes takes millions of years. It happens on the surface of the Earth and underground, where the Earth is very hot.

There are three kinds of rock, and they form in different ways. Igneous rock forms when **molten** rock cools down deep underground or on the Earth's surface. When rocks are heated, or heated under a lot of pressure, they change into metamorphic rock. Sedimentary rock is made of small pieces worn off other rocks packed together in layers.

The rock cycle

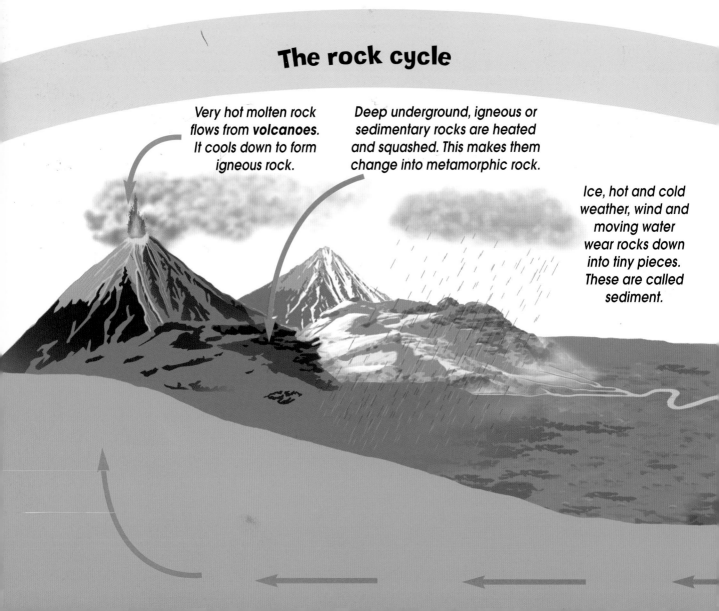

Very hot molten rock flows from **volcanoes**. It cools down to form igneous rock.

Deep underground, igneous or sedimentary rocks are heated and squashed. This makes them change into metamorphic rock.

Ice, hot and cold weather, wind and moving water wear rocks down into tiny pieces. These are called sediment.

Three types of rock

igneous rock
basalt

sedimentary rock
sandstone

metamorphic rock
marble

Rivers carry the sediment to the sea.

More sediment is formed from rocks along the coast. The sediment sinks to the seabed. It is squashed and forms sedimentary rock.

Sedimentary rock gets pushed further down by new layers of sediment. Deep underground, it melts into molten rock.

Igneous Rock: Granite

Granite is an igneous rock. This means it is formed of very hot molten rock from deep under the Earth's surface.

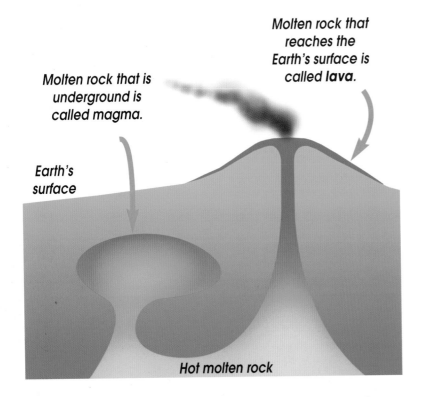

Molten rock that reaches the Earth's surface is called lava.

Molten rock that is underground is called magma.

Earth's surface

Hot molten rock

Sometimes the molten rock, or **magma**, bursts to the Earth's surface through a volcano. It cools down and hardens to form igneous rock.

The molten rock can also cool and harden under the Earth's surface.

Granite is formed from rock that cools down inside the Earth.

Granite landscape

This is granite on the Isle of Mull, Scotland. The red colour means this granite has a lot of feldspar in it. This granite was once inside the Earth. The Earth's outer layer has worn away, so now we can see the rocks.

Minerals in rocks

Like all rocks, granite is made from **minerals**. They are the tiny pieces of material that join together to form rocks. Minerals can be many different shapes and colours. Some minerals form as **crystals**.

Granite ingredients

Granite is made of three different minerals: quartz, mica and feldspar. They were all **welded** together when the granite formed.

Quartz (grey)

Mica (black)

Feldspar (pink)

Sedimentary Rock: Sandstone

Sandstone is a sedimentary rock. It is made up of many layers of sand. Sand is a type of rock, too. It is made up of minerals.

You can feel the grains when sand runs through your fingers.

You can look at individual **grains** of sand through a microscope. The grains are tiny pieces of a mineral called quartz. Sand is also made up of tiny pieces of animal shells or other minerals.

Sand grains through a microscope

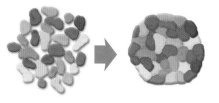

weight of new layers

squeezed layers

grains of sand

sedimentary rock

Ice, heat, cold, wind and moving water wear grains of sand off rocks. These pile up in layers. As more and more layers form, the layers at the bottom are squeezed together to form sandstone. This can happen in a desert, a river, or the sea.

Sandstone landscape

*In this photograph of sandstone. It is easy to see the many different layers of sand it is formed of. You can often find **fossils** in sandstone layers!*

All together, the grains of sand can form **dunes** on beaches or in deserts. Sand can also form in layers on the bottom of a river or the sea.

Metamorphic Rock: Gneiss

Gneiss (pronounced "nice") is a metamorphic rock. Rocks become metamorphic when they change and become a different kind of rock.

Deep under the Earth's surface, there is a lot of heat and pressure. The rocks there are heated and squeezed. This makes rocks change.

What happens when rocks change?

Rocks are made of minerals. This means that a rock changes when its minerals change. When you compare a rock before it has changed and afterwards, it can look quite different! Look what happens when granite turns into gneiss:

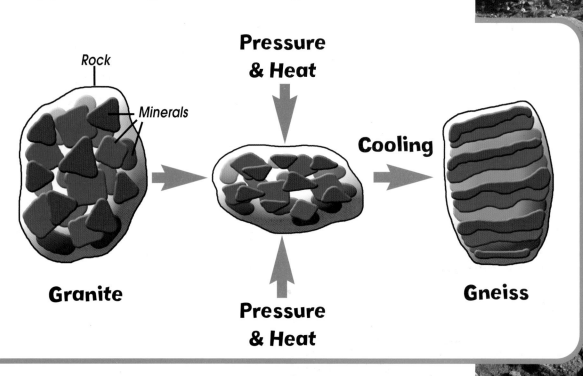

Rock

Minerals

Pressure & Heat

Cooling

Pressure & Heat

Granite

Gneiss

*Granite
(igneous rock)*

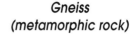

*Gneiss
(metamorphic rock)*

When you compare granite with gneiss, you can see that the pattern has changed. The minerals in granite are speckled. In gneiss, they look stripy!

Gneiss

Gneiss landscape

This is in a part of northern Canada called the Canadian Shield. It is an area that is mostly made of gneiss. This region is one of the largest areas of metamorphic rock on Earth. The rocks here are almost 3,000 million years old.

Amazing Rocky Places

Rivers, rain, ice and wind wear away at rocks until they crumble. This is called **weathering**. Sometimes rock is worn down and then carried away by wind, water or ice. This is called **erosion**.

It's a Fact!

Weathering and erosion make rock stacks, cliffs, canyons and arches like those on this page.

Grand Canyon, USA

This huge canyon was carved by a river. It took over 17 million years for it to form. It is made of sandstone and is up to 1.8 kilometres deep!

Monument Valley, USA

This huge area of red sandstone was formed about 270 million years ago! It has taken millions of years to wear it down to these shapes. The rock stacks you can see here are called spires.

Elephant's Arch, Italy

Here on the coast of Sicily, the sea has created this amazing natural arch. It is made of cooled lava.

Red lava, Iceland

These are huge lava hills. They are bright red because of the different forms of iron in them.

Rock Collector

Some igneous rocks you might find

Andesite

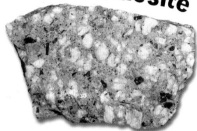

MINERALS: feldspar, mica, hornblende
FORMED: in volcanoes from lava
FEATURES: fine grains of grey-coloured crystals with some larger light and dark ones

Basalt

MINERALS: feldspar, augite
FORMED: in volcanoes from lava
FEATURES: dark colour, very fine grains of crystal, often full of tiny holes

Dolerite

MINERALS: feldspar, augite
FORMED: deep underground from magma
FEATURES: mostly dark with tiny speckles of light-coloured crystals

Gabbro

MINERALS: feldspar, augite
FORMED: deep underground from magma
FEATURES: many dark and some light-coloured crystals

Obsidian

MINERALS: quartz, feldspar
FORMED: in volcanoes from lava
FEATURES: like black glass, may have white 'snowflakes'

Porphyry

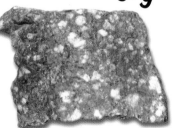

MINERALS: quartz, mica, feldspar
FORMED: deep underground from magma
FEATURES: a mix of some large crystals and many tiny ones

Diorite

MINERALS: feldspar, mica, hornblende
FORMED: deep underground from magma
FEATURES: speckled; large dark and
light crystals

Granite

MINERALS: quartz, mica, feldspar
FORMED: deep underground from magma
FEATURES: speckled; large crystals in pink,
white and dark grey or black

Rhyolite

MINERALS: quartz, feldspar
FORMED: in volcanoes from lava
FEATURES: hard with very sharp edges,
tiny light-coloured crystals

Getting Started

To collect rocks properly you will need the right tools. One of the most important tools is a rock hammer. It is very hard. Only hammer small, loose rocks with it.

You will also need:

- A strong rucksack for your tools and rock specimens.

- A notebook to write down where and when you found the specimens.

- A magnifying glass for looking at details.

- 'Bubble wrap' or newspaper to protect specimens.

- Goggles to wear when hammering. Rock splinters may fly about and get in your eyes.

Rock Collector

Some sedimentary rocks you might find

Arkose

MINERALS: quartz, feldspar
FORMED: in dry areas with **flash floods**
FEATURES: pink colour, made of large grains

Breccia

MINERALS: many minerals and rocks
(varies on where formed)
FORMED: at the foot of steep hillsides or cliffs
FEATURES: has large sharp pieces of rock

Coal

MINERALS: none; mainly made of carbon
FORMED: in vast swamp forests
FEATURES: black colour with shiny patches;
rubs off on your hands

Conglomerate

MINERALS: many minerals and rocks
(varies on where formed)
FORMED: seabeds, deserts and rivers
FEATURES: made of sand grains, and
pebbles of different kinds of rocks

Fossil limestone

MINERALS: calcite
FORMED: on the seabed
FEATURES: light colour, may contain fossils

Sandstone

MINERALS: quartz
FORMED: in shallow water, on seabeds
or riverbeds
FEATURES: made of small grains of sand;
smooth sandy surface

Chalk

MINERALS: calcite
FORMED: on the seabed
FEATURES: white and powdery, may rub off on your hands

Crinoidal limestone

MINERALS: calcite
FORMED: on the seabed
FEATURES: grey colour, packed with **crinoid** fossils

Shale

MINERALS: quartz, mica, feldspar
FORMED: on the seabed
FEATURES: dark colour with some light specks, made of tiny grains

Finding Rocks

You can find rocks in lots of places. The seashore, riverbanks and hillsides are all good places to look.

Always go rock collecting with an adult, because some places may be dangerous.

- Always ask permission to go on private land.
- Collect loose rock specimens. Do not break off large pieces.
- Use your rock hammer to break rocks into smaller pieces.
- Photograph locations and large features such as cliffs, hillsides and mountains.

Rock Collector

Some metamorphic rocks you might find

Eclogite

MINERALS: olivine, garnet, augite
FORMED: deep in the Earth's crust
FEATURES: mostly made up of red and green mineral crystals

Gneiss

MINERALS: quartz, feldspar, mica
FORMED: very deep under mountain ranges
FEATURES: bands of dark and light colours

Hornfels

MINERALS: quartz, mica, cordierite
FORMED: near large areas of igneous rock
FEATURES: dark colour, has very sharp edges

Mylonite

MINERALS: various, mainly quartz
FORMED: near **thrust faults**
FEATURES: thin layers of minerals; light-coloured quartz **veins**

Schist

MINERALS: quartz, mica, feldspar
FORMED: deep beneath mountains
FEATURES: wavy surface with a silvery shimmer

Serpentinite

MINERALS: pyroxene, garnet, hornblende, antigorite
FORMED: deep in the Earth's crust
FEATURES: bright red and dark green colours

Green marble

MINERALS: calcite
FORMED: in areas with igneous rock
FEATURES: very light colour with patches
of green

Metaquartzite

MINERALS: quartz
FORMED: near large areas of igneous rock
FEATURES: light quartz crystals; looks a bit
like a lump of sugar

Slate

MINERALS: quartz, mica, chlorite
FORMED: beneath mountains
FEATURES: can be broken into thin layers;
may contain crystals of pyrites

Displaying Rocks

When you start collecting rocks, you might want to display them, too. Here is some advice on how to start your very own rock display.

- Rocks can be heavy, so use a strong shelf or box for your display.

- Before displaying your rocks, make sure they have been cleaned.

- Use an old toothbrush and warm water to remove loose soil and dirt.

- Make neat card labels for each specimen, saying where it was found and the type of rock it is.

- Keep a record of all your specimens in a notebook or on your computer.

Record Breakers

Most common rock

Basalt covers the most area on Earth – almost 75 per cent! All ocean beds are made of this igneous rock.

This is Giant's Causeway in Ireland. It is made up of huge basalt columns that have naturally formed in this way.

Largest rock

The largest freestanding rock is Uluru in Australia. It is made of sandstone. Uluru is 348 metres high and over 3.6 kilometres long!

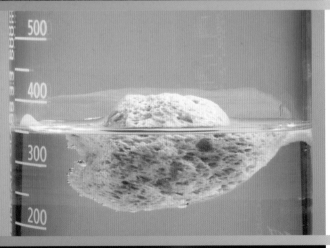

Lightest rock

The lightest rock is pumice. It is an igneous rock that is formed from lava froth and has many holes in it. This makes it light enough to float on water!

Oldest rock

The oldest rock that was formed on Earth is just over 4,000 million years old! It is a metamorphic rock called acasta gneiss.

Did You Know?

On Hawaii, the sand on some beaches is black! This is because the sand is made up of ground-up volcanic lava.

Sometimes you can find small rocks from Mars on Earth. They are broken off the surface of Mars by passing **asteroids**!

If you drilled deep enough into any of the Earth's landmasses, you would find granite or gneiss.

Limestone is a sedimentary rock. It is often used for building. The famous pyramids at Giza in Egypt are all built from limestone.

Obsidian is a black rock formed in volcanoes. When it breaks, its edges are so sharp that it has been used for knives and spears.

Marble is used for many statues and monuments. It is a metamorphic rock. The Leaning Tower of Pisa in Italy is made of marble.

Shiprock Pinnacle in New Mexico, USA, is a 500-metre-tall pillar of many types of igneous rock. It used to be the central part of a volcano.

Roads are made from very small rock chippings mixed with tar.

Some of the Moon's surface is made of basalt. This is a type of lava that is also common on Earth.

Glossary

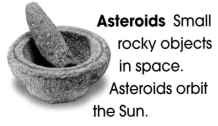

Asteroids Small rocky objects in space. Asteroids orbit the Sun.

Crinoid A sea creature that is related to starfish and sea urchins.

Crystals A crystal is a solid mineral form. It has straight edges and smooth faces.

Dunes Mounds of sand formed by the wind. You can find dunes on beaches and in deserts.

Erosion The wearing down and carrying away of rock by moving water, ice or wind.

Flash floods Sudden floods that happen when there are very strong rainfalls.

Fossil The shape or remains of a prehistoric plant or animal preserved in rock.

Grains All rocks are made of grains. They are the tiny crystals, or pieces of rock, which come together to form larger rocks.

Lava Molten rock on the Earth's surface which usually comes out of a volcano.

Magma Magma is molten rock when it is underground. Many igneous rocks, such as granite, are made when magma becomes hard.

Minerals The naturally formed materials that rocks are made of. Some rocks contain many different minerals.

Molten If a rock is molten, it means that it is extremely hot and flows like a liquid.

Thrust faults Places where one block of rock moves over another.

Veins Thin cracks running through rocks which are full of minerals.

Volcano A hole in the Earth's crust where molten rock bursts to the surface.

Weathering The wearing away of rocks without any movement. Frost, rain water and plant roots are examples of how weathering breaks rocks down.

Welded When two materials are welded, it means that they were joined together with heat or pressure.

Index

Copyright © ticktock Entertainment Ltd 2008
First published in Great Britain in 2008 by ticktock Media Ltd,
2 Orchard Business Centre, North Farm Road, Tunbridge Wells, Kent, TN2 3XF

ticktock project editor: Julia Adams
ticktock project designer: Emma Randall
ticktock picture researcher: Lizzie Knowles
series consultant: Terry Jennings

We would like to thank: Graham Rich, Sophie Furse, James Powell, Joe Harris

ISBN-13: 978 1 84696 694 1 pbk

Printed in China

Picture credits (t=top; b=bottom; c=centre; l=left; r=right):
age fotostock/ SuperStock: 14br. All Canada Photos/ Alamy: 12-13b. Tom Bean/ Corbis: 11br. Dea/ A.
Rizzi/ Getty Images: 21cr. iStock: 5bl, 22ft, 23tl, 23bl. Andrew J. Martinez/ Science Photo Library: 3D, 10tl.
Susumu Nishinaga/ Science Photo Library: 10br. Chris and Helen Pellant: 3E, F, G, H, 7tl, 7tr, 8b, 9bl x2,
12tl, 13t x2, 14tl, 15br, 16 all, 17l x3, 18 all, 19l x3, 19tr, 20 all, 21l x3. Shutterstock: OFC, 1, 2, 3A, B, C, I, J, K, 4
all, 5t, 5bc, 5br, 6tl, 7tc, 9ftl, 9tl, 9cl, 9cr, 10cl, 10-11c, 14-15 main, 14l, 17r x4, 19br x2, 21tr, 21br, 22t, 23tr, 23cl,
23cr, 23br, 24tl, OBC. Shiela Terry/ Science Photo Library: 22c.
ticktock Media Archive: 6-7b, 8c, 11tr, 12b, 22b.

Rock Stars

ROCKS

Chris and Helen Pellant